ALBERT TAPPER & PETER PRESS

A Guy Goes into a DOCTOR'S Office...

A Collection of Doctor Jokes

D1418306

MJF BOOKS
NEW YORK

Published by MJF Books
Fine Communications
322 Eighth Avenue
New York, NY 10001

A Guy Goes into a Doctor's Office...
LCCN 2003105952
ISBN 1-56731-586-0

Manufactured in the United States of America on acid-free paper ∞

MJF Books and the MJF colophon are trademarks of
Fine Creative Media, Inc.

QM   12   11   10   9   8   7   6   5   4   3   2   1

DEDICATIONS

To my good friend Norman, who only plays golf at the swankiest country club—mine! To my good friend Norman, who only stays in the best suite at the Hotel Carlyle—mine! To my good friend Norman, who always sits in the best seat at Fenway Park—mine! To my good friend Norman, whose gravestone when he passes on will read *"Here Lies Norman—GUEST OF..."*

A.T.

Because of the countless years spent on psychiatrists' couches trying desperately, but with no success, to deal with my narcissistic nature, I dedicate this book to myself.

P. P.

ACKNOWLEDGEMENTS

Our deepest appreciation to all who have contributed to this book. Jokes and suggestions came via the Internet, fax, telephone, and mail. We even had one contributor roll down the window of his car while traveling on the Major Deegan Expressway and flip three jokes wrapped around a golf ball through the open window of our van.

To our secretary, Joanne, who probably did more work than anyone else and got the least amount of credit.

We also wish to acknowledge Hippocrates, who made this book possible by starting it all.

A man goes to his doctor for a complete checkup. He hasn't been feeling well and wants to find out if he's ill. After the checkup the doctor comes out with the results of the examination.

"I'm afraid I have some bad news. You're dying, and you don't have much time," the doctor says.

"Oh no, that's terrible. How long have I got?" the man asks.

"Ten . . ." says the doctor.

"Ten? Ten what? Months? Weeks? What?!" the man asks desperately.

"Ten . . . nine . . . eight . . . seven . . ."

A Guy Goes into a Doctor's Office. . .

A man walks into a doctor's office. He has a cucumber up his nose, a carrot in his left ear, and a banana in his right ear.

"What's the matter with me?" he asks the doctor.

The doctor replies, "You're not eating properly."

A young woman went to her doctor complaining of pain.

"Where are you hurting?" asked the doctor.

"You have to help me. I hurt all over," said the woman.

"What do you mean, 'all over'?" asked the doctor. "Be a little more specific."

The woman touched her right knee with her index finger and yelled, "Ow, that hurts!" Then she touched her left cheek and again yelled, "Ouch! That hurts, too." Then she touched her right earlobe. "Ow, even THAT hurts," she cried.

The doctor regarded her thoughtfully for a moment and told her his diagnosis: "You have a broken finger."

A baseball manager who had an ulcer was in his physician's office for a checkup. "Remember," the doctor said, "don't get excited, don't get mad, and forget about baseball when you're off the field." Then he added, "By the way, how come you let the pitcher bat yesterday with the tying run on second and two men out in the ninth?"

"Doctor, are you sure I'm suffering from pneumonia? I heard once about a doctor treating someone with pneumonia—he finally died of typhus."

"Don't worry, it won't happen to you. If I treat someone with pneumonia, he will die of pneumonia."

A SHORT HISTORY OF MEDICINE:

"Doctor, I have an earache."

2000 B.C.   "Here, eat this root."

1000 B.C.   "That root is heathen. Say this prayer."

1850 A.D.   "That prayer is superstition. Drink this potion."

1940 A.D.   "That potion is snake oil. Swallow this pill."

1985 A.D.   "That pill is ineffective. Take this anti-biotic."

2000 A.D.   "That antibiotic is artificial. Here, eat this root!"

A pipe burst in a doctor's house. He called a plumber. The plumber arrived, unpacked his tools, did mysterious plumber-type things for a while, and handed the doctor a bill for $600.

The doctor exclaimed, "This is ridiculous! I don't even make that much as a doctor!"

The plumber quietly answered, "Neither did I when I was a doctor."

The surgeon general of the United States was paying a visit to one of the country's top hospitals. During his tour he passed a room where a male patient was masturbating.

"What's this?" exclaimed the surgeon general. "What is the meaning of this?"

The doctor leading the tour explained, "I apologize. This man has a very serious condition where his testicles rapidly fill with semen. If he doesn't do that three times a day, they will explode and he will die."

"Oh, I am sorry," said the surgeon general.

On the next floor they passed a room where a nurse was performing oral sex on a patient.

"Oh, my God!" the Surgeon General said, shocked. "What is going on in there?"

"Same problem, better health plan," replied the doctor.

A seven-year-old girl told her mom, "A boy in my class asked me to play Doctor."

"Oh, dear," the mother nervously sighed. "What happened, honey?"

"Nothing, he made me wait forty-five minutes and then double-billed the insurance company."

"The doctor said he would have me on my feet in two weeks."

"And did he?"

"Yes, I had to sell the car to pay the bill."

A woman calling Mount Sinai Hospital said, "Hello, I want to know if a patient is getting better."

The voice on the other end of the line said, "What is the patient's name and room number?"

She said, "Yes, darling! She's Sarah Finkel, in room 302."

The voice said, "Oh, yes. Mrs. Finkel is doing very well. In fact, she's had two full meals, her blood pressure is fine, she's going to be taken off the heart monitor in a couple of hours, and if she continues this improvement, her doctor is going to send her home Tuesday."

The woman said, "Thank God! That's wonderful! Oh! That's fantastic! That's wonderful news!"

The man on the phone said, "From your enthusiasm I take it you must be a family member or a very close friend!"

She said, "I'm Sarah Finkel in 302! My doctor doesn't tell me shit!"

An old fellow came into the hospital truly on death's door due to an infected gallbladder. The surgeon who removed the gallbladder was adamant that his patients be up and walking the day after surgery to help prevent blood clots forming in the leg veins. The nurses walked the patient in the hall as ordered, and after the third day the nurse told how he complained bitterly each time they did. The surgeon told them to keep walking him.

After a week the patient was ready to go. His children came to pick him up and thanked the surgeon profusely for what he had done for their father. The surgeon was pleased and appreciated the thanks, but told them that it was really a simple operation and they had been lucky to get him in time. "But Doctor, you don't understand," they said. "Dad hasn't walked in years!"

Three men died and arrived at the Pearly Gates. St. Peter asked the first man who he was. "My name is Dr. Jones. I pioneered and developed the techniques for open-heart surgery. Because of my work on earth, thousands of people all around the world have lived longer, healthier lives. Surely there is a place for me in heaven."

"Yes," St. Peter said, "come on in."

The second man approached and said, "St. Peter, my name is Dr. Smith. I pioneered and developed the techniques for treating premature babies. Today there are thousands of children in the world whose lives were saved at birth because of my work. Surely there is a place for me in heaven."

"Yes, come on in," said St. Peter. St. Peter asked the third man who he was. "My name is Mr. Johnson. I originated and developed the idea for HMOs. Because of my ideas on managed care and the efficiencies I developed, billions of dollars have been saved in the health care industry. Surely there is a place for me in heaven."

"Yes," said St. Peter, "come on in. But you can only stay three days."

Question: How is a hospital gown like insur-
            ance?
Answer: You're never as covered as you think
            you are.

A Guy Goes into a Doctor's Office. . .

Question: What does it mean when the doctor
                says you have six months to live?
Answer: You have five months to pay.

A man was brought to Mercy Hospital and taken in for coronary surgery. The operation went well and as the groggy man regained consciousness, he was reassured by a Sister of Mercy who was waiting by his bed.

"Mr. Smith, you're going to be just fine," said the nun, gently patting his hand. "We do need to know, however, how you intend to pay for your stay here. Are you covered by insurance?"

"No, I'm not," the man whispered hoarsely. "Can you pay in cash?" persisted the nun. "I'm afraid I cannot, Sister."

"Well, do you have any close relatives?" the nun asked. "Just my sister in New Mexico," he volunteered. "But she's a humble spinster nun."

"Oh, I must correct you, Mr. Smith. Nuns are not 'spinsters'. They are married to God." "Wonderful," said Mr. Smith. "In that case, please send the bill to my brother-in-law."

Question: When does a doctor suggest elective surgery?

Answer: When he's ready for a new sports car.

Question: How can you tell if you have a cheap
doctor?

Answer: He takes Fridays off to play miniature
golf.

A young girl suffering from severe headaches had tests run by her doctor. The doctor said, "I'm sorry, miss, but you have a massive brain tumor."

The girl started crying and said to her mom, "I'm only fifteen years old. I don't want to die."

The doctor said, "Well, there is an experimental technique for a brain transplant, but it's expensive and not covered by insurance."

The girl's mother said, "Don't worry, dear. How much does it cost?"

The doctor replied, "Well, a male brain is $1,000,000 and the female brain is $25,000."

The mom said, "No problem. But why is the male brain more expensive then the female brain?"

The doctor replied, "Because the female brain is USED!"

Jerry was removing some engine valves from a car when he spotted the famous heart surgeon Dr. Samuel Kaiser, who was standing off to the side waiting for the service manager. Jerry, who was somewhat of a loudmouth, shouted across the garage, "Hey Kaise. Is dat you? Come over here a minute."

The famous surgeon, a bit surprised, walked over to where Jerry was working on the car. Jerry, in a loud voice that all could hear, said argumentatively, "So, Mr. Fancy Doctor, look at this work. I, too, take valves out, grind 'em, put in new parts, and when I'm finished, this baby will purr like a kitten. So how come you get the big bucks, when you and me are doing basically the same work?" Dr. Kaiser shook his head and replied in a soft voice, "Try doing your work with the engine running."

CNN reported in a news bulletin today that a pregnant woman who has been in a coma for nine months following an automobile accident has given birth to twins: a baby girl and a baby boy. Awakening from her coma and learning that she had given birth to twins, she asked if names had already been given to them.

"Yes," her doctor informed her, "because we didn't know if you would ever come out of the coma. Your brother Henry gave them their names. "Oh, dear God," the woman moaned. "My brother Henry is the family idiot. What in the world did he name them?"

"He named the baby girl Denise," answered the physician. "Well, that's not so bad," the woman replied. "What did he name the baby boy?"

The physician responded regretfully, "Denephew."

One afternoon a man went to his doctor and told him that he hadn't been feeling well lately. The doctor examined the man, left the room, and came back with three different bottles of pills.

The doctor said, "Take the green pill with a big glass of water when you wake up. Take the blue pill with a big glass of water after you eat lunch. Then just before going to bed, take the red pill with another big glass of water."

Startled to be put on so much medicine, the man stammered, "Jeez, Doc, exactly what is my problem?"

The doctor replied, "You're not drinking enough water."

A guy goes into a psychiatrist's office and lies on the couch. The shrink says, "I've done all I can for you. The best thing would be for you to go back to school." "But why, Doc? I don't want to go to school." "Give me two reasons why you don't want to go to school." "One, all the kids hate me. Two, all the teachers hate me." "Oh! That's no reason," says the shrink. "Come on, you have to go to school!" He says, "Give me two good reasons WHY I should go to school!" The shrink thinks for a moment and then responds, "One, you are FIFTY-TWO years old. Two, you are the PRINCIPAL!"

A lady went to the doctor and complained that her husband was losing interest in sex. The doctor gave her a pill but warned her that it was still experimental. He told her to slip it in her husband's mashed potatoes at dinner, and so she did just that.

About a week later she returned to the doctor's office and said, "That pill worked great. I put it in my husband's mashed potatoes just like you said. It wasn't five minutes later, and he jumped up, raked all the food and dishes on the floor, grabbed me, ripped all my clothes off, and ravished me right there on the table!" The doctor said, "I'm sorry, we didn't realize that the pill was that strong. We will be glad to pay for any damages."

The lady replied, "Naah. That's okay. We aren't going back to Denny's anyway."

One morning a doctor and his wife were having a very heated argument over breakfast. As he stormed out of the house on his way to the clinic, the angry doctor yelled to his wife, "You aren't that good in bed either!"

By mid-morning he decided that he had better make amends and phoned home. After many rings his wife, clearly out of breath, answered the phone. "What took you so long to answer, and why are you panting?"

The wife replied, "I was in bed."

Then the doctor asked, "What in the world are you doing in bed at this hour?"

His wife responded, "Getting a second opinion."

A cardiologist died and was given an elaborate funeral.

A huge heart covered in flowers stood behind the casket during the service. Following the eulogy, the heart opened, and casket the rolled inside. The heart then closed, sealing the doctor in the beautiful heart forever. There wasn't a dry eye in the audience.

At that point, one of the mourners burst into laughter.

When confronted he said, "I'm sorry, I was just thinking of my own funeral . . . I'm a gynecologist."

At that point, the proctologist fainted.

"Doctor, Doctor, you've got to help me—I just can't stop my hands from shaking!"

"Do you drink a lot?"

"Not really—I spill most of it!"

"Doctor, Doctor, will I be able to play the violin after the operation?"

"Yes, of course."

"Great! I never could before!"

A man visits his doctor because he has a severe stuttering problem. After a thorough examination the doctor consults with the patient.

Doctor: "It appears that your penis is about six inches too long and is pulling on your vocal cords, thereby causing you this annoying problem of stuttering."

Patient: "Ddddocttor. Whhaaat cccan I dddo?"

The doctor scratches his forehead, thinks for a minute, and says "There is a procedure whereby we can free up the strain on the vocal cords by removing that six inches from the penis, freeing you from this horrible problem."

The patient, stuttering badly, states that this problem has caused him so much embarrassment and loss of employment that anything would be worth it. The doctor plans for the procedure. The operation is a success and six months later the patient comes in for his follow-up.

Patient: "Doctor, I have not stuttered since the operation. I have a great new job and my self-esteem is fantastic. However, there is one problem. My wife says that she sort of misses the great sex we used to have before the extra six inches were removed. So I was wondering if it is possible to reattach those six inches?"

The doctor scratches his forehead, thinks for a minute, and says, "I dddooonn't ttthhhinkkkk thattt wooould bbbbe posssssibbble."

A guy goes into a doctor's office and the doctor asks him if things have gotten better for him since he and his wife got divorced. The guy says, "Well, I did what you told me to do to relieve the stress caused by my marriage. First, I pictured myself next to a stream with birds singing in the crisp cool mountain air. Nothing bothered me there. No one knew this secret place. I was in total seclusion from that place called 'the world'. The soothing sound of a gentle waterfall filled the air with a cascade of serenity. But it didn't help. I kept seeing her face and got more and more upset." The doctor says, "Was the water clear?" The guy says, "Clear as crystal." "Good," says the doctor. "Now, can you close your eyes and make out the face of the person whose head you're holding under the water?" "Oh, God!" says the guy. "It's my wife." The doctor smiles and says, "There now, feeling better?"

A woman accompanied her husband to the doctor's office. After his checkup the doctor called the wife into his office alone. He said, "Your husband is suffering from a very severe disease, combined with horrible stress. If you don't do the following your husband will surely die: Each morning fix him a healthy breakfast. Be pleasant and make sure he is in a good mood. For lunch make him a nutritious meal. For dinner prepare an especially nice meal for him. Don't burden him with chores, as he probably had a hard day. Don't discuss your problems with him, it will only make his stress worse. And most importantly, make love with your husband several times a week and satisfy his every whim. If you can do this for the next ten months to a year, I think your husband will regain his health completely."

On the way home the husband asked his wife, "What did the doctor say?" "You're going to die," she replied.

A man speaks frantically into the phone, "My wife is pregnant and her contractions are only two minutes apart!"

"Is this her first child?" the doctor queries.

"No, you idiot!" the man shouts. "This is her husband!"

A man was in an accident, and unfortunately his penis was chopped off. The victim was rushed to the hospital, where the doctor examined him.

After careful examination the doctor said, "We can replace it with a small size for $2,000, a medium size for $5,000, or an extra-large size for $10,000. I realize it's a lot of money, so take your time and talk it over with your wife."

When the doctor came back into the room he found the man staring sadly at the floor. "We've decided," the man told him as he choked back tears. "My wife says that she'd rather have a new kitchen."

A Guy Goes into a Doctor's Office. . .

A young doctor had just opened his office and felt really excited. His secretary told him a man was there to see him. The young doctor told her to send him in.

Pretending to be a busy doctor, he picked up the phone just as the man came in. "Yes, that's right. The fee is $200. Yes, I'll expect you at 2:00 and no later—I'm a very busy man."

He hung up and turned to the man waiting. "May I help you?" "No," said the man, "I just came in to install the phone."

A man needing a heart transplant is told by his doctor that the only heart available is that of a sheep. The man finally agrees and the doctor transplants the sheep heart into the man.

A few days after the operation the man comes in for a checkup.

The doctor asks him, "How are you feeling?"

The man replies, "Not BAAAD!"

A middle-aged woman had a heart attack and was taken to the hospital. While on the operating table she had a near-death experience. Seeing God she asked, "Is my time up?" God answered, "No, you have another forty years, two months and eight days to live."

Upon recovery the woman decided to stay in the hospital and have a facelift, liposuction, and a tummy tuck. She even had someone come in and change her hair color. Since she had so much more time to live, she figured she might as well make the most of it.

After her last operation she was released from the hospital. While crossing the street on her way home, she was hit by a car and died immediately.

Arriving in front of God she demanded, "I thought you said I had another forty years—why didn't you pull me out of the path of the car?"

God replied, "I didn't recognize you."

At a medical convention, a male doctor and a female doctor start eyeing each other. The male doctor asks the female doctor to dinner and she accepts. As they sit down at the restaurant she excuses herself to go and wash her hands.

After dinner, one thing leads to another and they end up in her hotel room. Just as things are getting hot, the female doctor interrupts and says she has to go and wash her hands. Once she comes back, they go for it. Afterward, she gets up and says she is going to wash her hands.

As she comes back, the male doctor says, "I bet you are a surgeon." She confirms and asks how he knew.

"Easy—you're always washing your hands."

She then says, "I bet you're an anesthesiologist."

"Wow, how did you guess?" he asks.

She replies, "I didn't feel a thing."

A guy goes into a psychiatrist's office. He's a world-class jockey who had once ridden a winner of the Kentucky Derby. The psychiatrist realizes that because of the jockey's occupation, he suffers from emotional extremes: winning one race, losing the next and so on. The shrink wants to determine the jockey's capacity to understand emotions, so he asks him, "What is the opposite of joy?" "Sadness," comes the answer. "And the opposite of depression?" "Elation." Again the psychiatrist was pleased and asked, "How about the opposite of woe?" "I believe that would be giddyup," the jockey replied.

A Guy Goes into a Doctor's Office...

Three doctors are in a duck blind and a bird flies overhead. The general practitioner looks at it and says, "Looks like a duck, flies like a duck . . . it must be a duck." He shoots at it but misses, and the bird flies away.

The next bird flies overhead, and the pathologist looks at it, then looks through the pages of a bird manual, and says, "Hmmm . . . green wings, yellow bill, quacking sound . . . must be a duck." He raises his gun to shoot it, but the bird is long gone.

A third bird flies over. The surgeon raises his gun and shoots almost without looking, brings the bird down, and turns to the pathologist and says, "Go see if that was a duck."

Morris complained to his friend Irving that love-making with his wife was becoming routine and boring.

"Get creative, Morris. Break up the monotony. Why don't you try 'playing Doctor' for an hour? That's what I do," said Irving.

"Sounds great," Morris replied, "but how do you make it last for an hour?"

"Just keep her in the waiting room for fifty-five minutes!"

A Guy Goes into a Doctor's Office. . .

In Ireland there is a mental institution that every year picks two of its most reformed patients and questions them. If they get the questions right, they are free to leave.

This year the two lucky gents were Paddy and Mike. They were called down to the office and left there by the orderly. They were told to wait as the doctor got their files. The doctor came out and motioned for Paddy to come in for his questioning. When Paddy came into the office he was instructed to sit in the seat across from the doctor.

"Paddy, you know the tradition of this institution, so I imagine you know why you are here. You will be asked two questions, and if you get them right, you will be free to go. Do you understand all that you have been told?" asked the doctor. Paddy nodded, and the doctor began to question him. The first question was this: "Paddy, if you were to poke out one of your eyes, what would happen?"

"I would be half blind of course," Paddy answered immediately.

"What would happen if I poked out the other eye?"

"I would be completely blind," said Paddy, knowing that he had just gotten his freedom. The doctor then sent him outside while he drew up the paperwork and retrieved Mike's files.

When Paddy got back to the waiting room however, he told Mike what the questions would be and what the correct answers were.

The doctor called in Mike and followed the same procedure that he had with Patty. "Mike, the first question is, what would happen if you cut off one of your ears?"

"I would be blind in one eye," Mike said, remembering what he had been told. The doctor wrote a big "X" in his file and asked the next question. "Mike, what would happen if I cut off your other ear?"

"I would be completely blind," Mike answered with a smile as if he knew he had passed.

The doctor put another "X" in his file but figured he'd give Mike one more chance to win his freedom. He asked what his reasoning was, and he said flatly, "Me hat would fall down over me eyes."

A Guy Goes into a Doctor's Office. . .

A guy goes into a psychiatrist's office and says that he is George Washington. He finishes up the session by telling the shrink, "Tomorrow we will cross the Delaware and surprise them when they least expect it." As soon as the appointment is over, the psychiatrist picks up the phone and says, "King George, this is Benedict Arnold. I have the plans."

"I'm afraid I have bad news," a doctor told his anxious patient. "You only have six months to live."

The patient sat in stunned silence for the next several minutes. Regaining his composure, he apologetically told his physician that he had no medical insurance. "I can't possibly pay you in that time."

"OK," the doctor said, "let's make it nine months."

During her annual checkup an attractive young woman was asked to disrobe and climb onto the examining table.

"Doctor," she replied shyly, "I just can't undress in front of you."

"Alright," said the physician, "I'll flick off the lights. You undress and tell me when you're through."

In a few moments, her voice rang out in the darkness, "Doctor, I've undressed. What shall I do with my clothes?"

"Put them on the chair, on top of mine."

A doctor had just finished making love to one of his patients. He was resting afterwards and was feeling a bit guilty because he thought it wasn't really ethical for a doctor to screw one of his patients.

However, a little voice in his head said, "Lots of other doctors have sex with their patients so it's not like you're the first. . . ." This made the doctor feel a bit better until another voice in his head said, "... but they probably weren't veterinarians."

A doctor was hurrying down the hallway when a nurse came rushing after him, explaining that she needed his signature on a patient's chart.

He reached into his pocket and was about to sign his name when he realized he was holding a rectal thermometer. "Damn!" he says to the nurse. "Some asshole has got my favorite pen!"

A married couple went to the hospital to have their baby delivered. Upon their arrival, the doctor said he had invented a new machine that would transfer a portion of the mother's labor pain to the father. He asked if they were willing to try it out. They were both very much in favor of it. The doctor set the knob to 10% for starters, explaining that even 10% was probably more pain than the father had ever experienced before. But as labor progressed, the husband felt fine, so he asked the doctor to go ahead and bump it up a notch. The doctor then adjusted the machine to 20% pain transfer. The husband was still feeling fine. The doctor checked the husband's blood pressure and pulse and was amazed at how well he was doing. At this, they decided to try for 50%. The husband continued to feel quite well. Since it was obviously helping out his wife considerably, he encouraged the doctor to transfer ALL the pain to him. The wife delivered a healthy baby with virtually no pain. She and her husband were ecstatic. When they got home, they found the mailman dead on their porch.

The census taker was greeted at the door by six-year-old Susie. She told him that her daddy was a doctor but he wasn't home because he was performing an appendectomy.

"Goodness, that's a very big word for such a little girl," the census taker said. "Do you know what it means?"

"Uh-huh," Susie replied. "Two thousand bucks, and that doesn't even include the anesthesiologist!"

A patient was looking a little worried when the doctor came in to administer his annual physical, so the first thing the doctor did was to ask whether anything was troubling him.

"Well, to tell the truth, Doc, yes," answered the patient. "You see, I seem to be getting forgetful. I'm never sure where I put the car, or whether I answered a letter, or where I'm going, or what it is I'm going to do once I get there—if I get there. So, I really need your help. What can I do?"

The doctor mused for a moment, then answered in his kindest tone, "Pay me in advance."

A Guy Goes into a Doctor's Office. . .

A well-respected surgeon was relaxing on his sofa one evening just after arriving home from work. As he was tuning into the evening news, the phone rang. The doctor calmly answered it and heard the familiar voice of a colleague on the other end of the line.

"We need a fourth for poker," said the friend.

"I'll be right over," whispered the doctor.

As he was putting on his coat, his wife asked, "Is it serious?"

"Oh, yes, quite serious," said the doctor gravely. "In fact, three doctors are there already."

A guy goes into a psychiatrist's office looking as if the weight of world were on his shoulders. When he's settled comfortably on the couch, the psychiatrist begins his therapy session. "I'm not aware of your problem," the doctor says, "so perhaps you should start at the very beginning." "Of course," replied the patient. "In the beginning, I created the Heavens and the Earth . . ."

A guy goes into a psychiatrist's office. "Doc!" the man screams, "I've lost my memory!" "When did this happen?" asks the psychiatrist. The man looks at him and says, "When did what happen?"

A guy goes into a doctor's office and the doctor is sitting there with a somber look on his face. He says to the patient, "I have some bad news and some very bad news." The patient says, "Well, might as well give me the bad news first." The doctor says, "The lab called with your test results and it seems that you have only twenty-four hours to live." With that news the patient jumps over the couch in shock and says, "TWENTY-FOUR HOURS! That's terrible!! WHAT could be WORSE? What's the very bad news?" The doctor says, "I've been trying to reach you since yesterday."

A Guy Goes into a Doctor's Office. . .

A guy goes into a psychiatrist's office and says, "Once I had multiple personalities, but now we are feeling well."

A guy goes into a doctor's office and says, "Doctor, I have a tendency to get fat in certain places. What would you recommend?" The doc thinks for a moment and says, "Stay out of those places!"

A guy goes into a psychiatrist's office and tells the shrink that everyone hates him. "Nonsense," says the shrink, "But tell me why you think everyone hates you." "For starters," says the patient, "I'm black." "That's no reason to be hated," says the shrink. "That's true," says the man on the couch, "but you see, I am also a homosexual." "Again," says the shrink, "that's no reason for people to hate you." "True," says the patient, "but then, I am also a lawyer." "Ah," says the shrink, "now we're getting somewhere."

A Guy Goes into a Doctor's Office. . .

A guy goes into a doctor's office because of severe problems with his sex life. The doctor asks a lot of questions, but doesn't seem to be getting a clear picture of the problem. Finally, he asks, "Do you ever watch your girlfriend's face while you're having sex?" "Well, yes, I did once," says the patient. "Well, how did she look?" "Oh, boy . . . she looked VERY angry!" At this point the doctor says, "Now, tell me, you say that you have only seen your girlfriend's face once during sex; that seems somewhat unusual. How did it occur that you saw her face that time?" "She was watching us through the window."

A Guy Goes into a Doctor's Office. . .

A guy goes into a doctor's office with his wife in tow. The doctor asks, "Fred, how was the memory clinic you went to last month?" "Outstanding," Fred replies. "They taught us all the latest psychological techniques—visualization, association—it made a huge difference for me." "That's great! What was the name of the clinic?" Fred goes blank. He thinks and thinks but can't remember. Then a smile breaks across his face and he asks, "What do you call that red flower with the long stem and thorns?" The doctor says, "You mean a rose?" "Yes, that's it!" He turns to his wife. "Rose, what was the name of that clinic?"

A guy goes into a doctor's office and says, "Doctor, you must help me. I'm under such a lot of stress, I keep losing my temper with people." The doc says, "Calm down and tell me about your problem." "I JUST DID, DIDN'T I, YOU STUPID BASTARD?!"

A guy goes into a doctor's office and the doctor walks in, sits down, and, with a long sigh, says to the guy, "I've got two pieces of bad news for you." The guy says, "What are they?" The doc says, "You have cancer." "Oh, my God," says the guy. "What's the other bad news?" "You also have Alzheimer's," answers the doctor. "Well," the guy says, "it could be worse—I could have cancer."

After undergoing a long and complicated operation, a patient kept complaining about a bump on his head and a horrible headache. Since his surgery had been an intestinal one, the nurse couldn't understand why he would be complaining about an aching head. Fearing that perhaps he may be suffering from some form of post-surgery shock, she decided to ask the surgeon who performed the operation.

"There's nothing to worry about, nurse," explained the surgeon. "He actually does have a bump on his head. Halfway through the operation we ran out of anesthetic."

A Guy Goes into a Doctor's Office. . .

A guy goes into a doctor's office completely bewildered by events he experienced in a recent trip to Vienna, Austria. The doctor says, "Calm down and tell me about it. I'm sure we can find some reasonable explanation." So the guy begins his story. It seems that a week earlier, as a tourist in Vienna, he was going through a graveyard and all of a sudden he heard music. No one was around, so he started searching for the source. He finally located the origin and found that it was coming from a grave with a headstone that read: "Ludwig van Beethoven, 1770–1827". Then he realized that the music was the Ninth Symphony—played backward! Puzzled, he left the graveyard and persuaded a friend to return with him. By the time they arrived back at the grave, the music had changed. This time it was the Seventh Symphony, but like the previous piece, it was being played backward. Curious, the two men agreed to consult a music scholar. When they returned with the expert, the Fifth Symphony was playing, again backward. The expert noticed that the symphonies were being played in the reverse order in which they were composed, the eighth, then the seventh, then the fifth.

By the next day the word had spread, and a throng had gathered around the grave. They were all listening to the Second Symphony being played backward.

"So, that's the story, Doc," the guy says, "and it's really driving me crazy." The doctor thinks for a moment; then a smile crosses his face. "Oh, I know what happened—he's decomposing."

A guy goes into a psychiatrist's office and says, "Doc, I got a real problem, I can't stop thinking about sex." The psychiatrist says, "Well, let's see what we can find out," and pulls out his ink blots. "What is this a picture of?" he asks. The man turns the picture upside down, then turns it around and states, "That's a man and a woman on a bed making love." The shrink says, "Very interesting," and shows the next picture. "And what is this a picture of?" The man looks and turns it in different directions and says, "That's a man and a woman on a bed making love." The therapist tries again with the third ink blot and asks the same question, "What is this a picture of?" The patient again turns it in all directions and replies, "That's a man and a woman on a bed making love."

The psychiatrist states, "Well, yes, you do seem to be obsessed with sex." "Me!?" cries the patient. "You're the one who keeps showing me the dirty pictures!"

A Guy Goes into a Doctor's Office. . .

A guy goes into a doctor's office. It's his first appointment and he wants to discuss how much the doctor plans to charge him, so he says to the doc, "What is your least expensive fee?" The doctor says, "$50 for three questions." The guy says, "That's pretty expensive, isn't it?" Wherein the doc replies, "Yes, so what's your third question?"

A Guy Goes into a Doctor's Office. . .

Little Johnny goes to see his pediatrician. The doctor thinks Johnny has a problem with simple deductive reasoning, so he says, "I have a word problem. There are three crows sitting on a farmer's fence. The farmer comes out and shoots one dead. How many crows are left?"

Johnny thinks and thinks and finally says, "Well, there would be none left!" The doctor looks at him and says, "Well, how do you figure?" Johnny says, "The shot would scare the other two crows away." The doctor, impressed, says, "Well, actually the answer is two, but I like the way you think."

Johnny returns to the doctor's office for his follow-up appointment. "Doc, I have a word problem for you. There are three women sitting on a park bench: one is sucking an ice cream, one is licking an ice cream, and the other is biting an ice cream. Which one is married?"

The doctor thinks and thinks and finally says, "It would be the one sucking the ice cream."

Johnny says, "No, it's the one with the ring on her finger, but I like the way you think!"

A Guy Goes into a Doctor's Office. . .

A guy goes into a doctor's office. He's very shy and he's had limited sexual experience. He tells the doctor that he's been seeing this girl for a while and she's really hot. He says to the doctor, "I think tonight's the night. We're having dinner with her parents, and then we're going out. And I've got a feeling I'm gonna get lucky after that." The doc says, "Be careful and don't forget to use a condom." He then pats the guy on the back and wishes him good luck.

Later that evening, when the guy sits down to dinner with his girlfriend and her parents, he breaks out in a sweat. He asks if he might give the blessing over the bread and they agree. He begins the prayer, but continues praying and praying, NEVER LOOKING UP. The girlfriend leans over and says, "You never told me that you were such a religious person." He leans back to her and says, "You never told me that your father is a doctor."

A guy goes into the office of a doctor who just happens to be his dearest pal. The guy has been feeling poorly lately and thinks his friend, the doctor, could prescribe some medication. The doctor writes out a prescription. The patient shakes the doctor's hand in gratitude and says, "Since we are the best of friends, I would not want to insult you by offering you payment, but I would like for you to know that I've mentioned you in my will." "That is very kind of you," says the doctor emotionally, and then adds, "Can I see that prescription I just gave you? I'd like to make a little change . . ."

A Guy Goes into a Doctor's Office. . .

A guy goes into a doctor's office and the doc, after carefully examining the guy, says, "You know, you're overweight." The man says, "I want a second opinion!"

"OK, you're ugly, too!"

A guy goes into a psychiatrist's office and is told by the shrink that his therapy is completed and that he is cured and ready to resume a normal life. The doctor asks the guy, "Now that you're emotionally healthy, do you have any idea what you might do?" The guy thinks for a moment, then replies, "Well, I went to school for mechanical engineering. That's still a good field, good money there. But on the other hand, I thought I might write a book about my experience here in therapy, what's it's like to be a patient. People might be interested in reading a book like that. In addition, I thought I might go back to college and study art history, which I've grown interested in lately." The psychiatrist nods and says, "Yes, those all sound like intriguing possibilities." The guy replies, "And the best part is, in my spare time, I can go on being a teapot."

How many psychiatrists does it take to change a light bulb?

Just one, but the light really has to want to change,

(or)

Just one, but it takes nine visits,

(or)

None. The light bulb will change when it's ready.

Doctor, Doctor, I've only got fifty-nine seconds to live!

Wait a minute, please.

On a train to a conference dealing with malpractice insurance, there were a bunch of doctors and a bunch of lawyers. Each of the doctors had a ticket. The group of lawyers had only ONE ticket for all of them. The doctors laughed, thinking the lawyers would get thrown off the train. When one of the lawyers, the lookout, said, "Here comes the conductor," all of the lawyers went into the bathroom. The doctors were puzzled.

The conductor came along and said, "Tickets, please," taking tickets from all of the doctors. He then knocked on the bathroom door and said, "Ticket, please." The lawyers slid their one ticket under the door. The conductor took it and moved on. The doctors felt really stupid.

On the way back from the conference, the doctors decided that they would try the same method. They bought one ticket for the whole group. They met up with the lawyers on the same train.

Again, the doctors snickered at the lawyers, but this time NONE of the lawyers had tickets. When the lookout said, "Conductor coming!" all the lawyers went to one bathroom and the doctors went to the other bathroom.

Before the conductor came on board, one of the lawyers left their bathroom, knocked on the doctor's bathroom, and said, "Ticket, please."

The doctor called Mrs. Green, saying, "Mrs. Green, your check came back." Mrs. Green answered, "So did my arthritis."

A guy goes into a mental hospital and asks,
"Who's in room 24?"
"Nobody," the doctor replies.
"Good," says the man, "I must have escaped."

A man complained to his friend, "My elbow hurts. I better go to the doctor." "Don't do that," volunteered his friend, "there's a new computer at the drug store that can diagnose any problem quicker and cheaper than a doctor. All you have to do is put in a urine sample, deposit $10, then the computer will give you your diagnosis and plan of treatment."

The man figured he had nothing to lose, so he took a sample of urine down to the drug store. Finding the machine, he poured in the urine and deposited the $10. The machine began to buzz and various lights flashed on and off. After a short pause a slip of paper popped out on which was printed:

You have tennis elbow. Soak your arm in warm water twice a day. Avoid heavy labor. Your elbow will be better in two weeks.

That evening as the man contemplated this breakthrough in medical science, he began to suspect fraud. To test his theory he mixed together some tap water, a stool sample from his dog, and urine samples from his wife and teenage daughter. To top it all off, he masturbated into the jar.

He took his concoction down to the drug store, poured it in the machine, and deposited $10. The machine went through the same buzzing and flashing routine as before then printed out the following message:

Your tap water has lead.

Get a filter.

Your dog has worms.

Give him vitamins.

Your daughter is on drugs.

Get her in rehab.

Your wife is pregnant.

It's not your baby.

Get a lawyer.

And if you don't stop jerking off, your tennis elbow will never get better.

A sixty-five-year-old woman is naked, jumping up and down on her bed, laughing and singing. Her husband walks into the bedroom and sees her. He watches her awhile then says, "You look ridiculous, what on earth are you doing?"

She says, "I just got my check-up and my doctor says I have the breasts of an eighteen-year-old." She starts laughing and jumping again. He says, "Yeah, right. And what did he say about your sixty-five-year old ass?"

She says, "Well, your name never came up."

Having grown tired of his career, a gynecologist decided to make a change and become a mechanic. He signed up for evening classes at his local tech college, attended faithfully, and learned all that he could.

As the time for the practical exam approached, he carefully prepared for weeks and passed the exam with remarkable skill.

When he received his results, he was shocked to see that he had been given a grade of 150%. Fearing an error may have been made, he spoke with the instructor.

"I don't wish to appear ungrateful for such an outstanding mark, but I was wondering if there had been an error which might need adjusting," he said.

"During the exam you took the engine apart perfectly," replied the instructor. "That was worth 50% of the total mark. You put the engine back together again perfectly, which was also worth 50% of the mark. The extra 50% I gave you because you did all of it through the MUFFLER!"

A young woman having a physical examination felt very embarrassed because of a weight problem. As she removed her last bit of clothing, she said, "Doctor, I feel so ashamed and embarrassed. I guess I've really let myself go."

"Now, now," the doctor said as he began to examine her. "Don't feel that way. You really don't look that bad."

"Do you really think so?" she asked.

"Of course," replies the doctor as he held a tongue depressor in front of her face. "Now open wide and say 'moo'!"

A woman went to her doctor and told him she would like to have some birth control pills.

Surprised by her request, the doctor said to her, "Pardon me, Mrs. Jones, but you're fifty-two years old. I don't think you need birth control pills."

"They help me sleep, doctor," she explained.

Now very confused, the doctor asked, "I don't understand, Mrs. Jones. How would birth control pills help you to sleep?"

Mrs. Jones replied, "Each morning I put one in my daughter's orange juice and I sleep much better at night."

A very drunk man looking for a whorehouse staggers into a podiatrist's office instead and weaves his way over to the receptionist.

Without bothering to look up, she waves him over to the examination bed and says, "Just stick it through the curtain."

Hoping something kinky is about to happen, the drunk pulls out his penis and sticks it through the crack in the curtain.

"That's not a foot!" the podiatrist screams.

"Holy shit, lady," the drunk replies, "I didn't know you had a minimum."

A guy goes into a doctor's office suffering from impotence. The doctor suggests a revolutionary new injection made from monkey genes. Willing to give it a try, the man is given the injection.

Much to the man's delight, it works. Nine months later his wife gives birth.

When the nurse comes out of the delivery room to give him the news, the man excitedly asks, "Is it a boy or a girl?"

The nurse replies, "We won't know for sure until it comes down from the chandelier."

After completing a patient's checkup, the proctologist begged him for some help.

"Could you help me out?" the doctor pleaded. "Could you let out a few loud, blood-curdling screams?"

"Why, Doc?" the patient asked. "It wasn't all that bad this time."

"The waiting room is packed with people right now," the proctologist explained, "and I don't want to miss my tee-off time."

"**D**oc, I can't seem to sleep anymore," Bill complained. "I've tried everything, but all I do is toss and turn."

"You must learn to relax," the doctor advised. "Try putting each part of your body to sleep separately."

That night Bill crawled into bed, got comfortable, and began talking to his body. "Toes, go to sleep," he whispered. "Feet, go to sleep. Legs, go to sleep. Hips, go to sleep. Stomach, go to sleep."

Just then his wife walked in wearing a transparent negligee.

Bill opened one eye, then lifted his head from the pillow. "OK," he shouted, "up, everybody . . . up!"

A man confided to his doctor that he had grown tired of his wife and wished there was a way of doing her in so he could have some good years left to himself.

"Make love to her every single day for a year," the doctor advised. "She'll never make it!"

A year later the doctor stopped by the man's house. He found the man sitting on the porch, looking thin and frail. The doctor could see the wife out back, splitting wood and looking very tanned and robust.

"Hello, Harry, you're looking good," said the doctor uneasily, "and Jenny certainly is the picture of health."

"Yeah, but little does she know," hissed Harry with an evil grin, "that tomorrow she dies!"

A woman wants to have bigger breasts, so she goes to see a plastic surgeon. The doctor tells her that she could either have implants or wear a special bra. The doctor explains, "When you flap your arms up and down, the bra will inflate."

This sounds like a much easier process than the implants, so she chooses the bra.

The next day she decides to try the bra out, so she goes to a bar. She sees a very attractive man sitting there. Flapping her arms, she strolls over to flirt with him and he promptly starts flapping his legs.

"I see we have the same doctor," he says.

While honeymooning on Cape Cod, two newly-weds decided to visit a historic graveyard.

As they were strolling through the graveyard, the mood struck them. They looked around and, not seeing anyone, stripped off their clothes and went at it hot and heavy on a tomb.

The following day the wife's back was aching from the adventure, so she went to see a doctor.

"Just how old are you, my dear?" the doctor asked.

"I'm twenty-five," replied the woman. "Why do you ask?"

"Because on your backside it says you died in 1819!" the doctor replied.

An elderly man went to the doctor for an annual physical. While listening to the old man's heart with his stethoscope, the doctor muttered, "Uh-oh!"

"What is it, Doctor?" the old man asked.

"Well, you appear to have a serious heart murmur. Do you smoke?" asked the doctor.

"Nope, never have," the old man replied.

"Do you drink excessively?" the doctor asked.

"Nope, never touch the stuff," said the old man.

"What about sex? Do you have a sex life?' the doctor inquired.

"Yes, I do!" the old man answered nervously.

"Well," the doctor said, "I'm afraid that with this heart murmur you're going to have to give up half of your sex life."

"Which half would that be, Doctor?" asked the old man. "The thinking or the looking?"

A Guy Goes into a Doctor's Office. . .

A guy goes into a doctor's office suffering from a terrible cold. The doctor prescribes some pills for him, but they don't help.

The guy goes back to the doctor the next day and this time he is given a shot, but that doesn't seem to help either.

Once again, the guy goes back to the doctor. This time he is told to go home and take a hot bath, and as soon as he finishes bathing he is to throw open all the windows and stand in the draft.

"What!" the guy exclaims. "If I do something like that, I'll end up with pneumonia!"

"That, I can cure!" says the doctor.

A guy goes into a psychiatrist's office with a pan-cake on his head, fried eggs on each shoulder, and a strip of bacon over each ear. The shrink, humoring him, asks, "What seems to be the problem?" The guy answers, "Doc, I'm worried about my brother."

Pregnant with her first child, Mary was at her obstetrician's for a check-up.

After the exam she shyly said to the doctor, "My husband would like to know . . ."

Before she could finish the sentence, the doctor placed a reassuring hand on her shoulder and said, "I know, I know. That is one question I get asked all the time. Yes, sex is fine until late in the pregnancy."

"No, doctor, that's not it," said an embarrassed Mary.

"Oh, then what is it?" the doctor asked.

"He'd like to know if I can still mow the lawn!"

A sixty-year-old man went to his doctor for a checkup. "You're in great shape," the doctor told him. "There's nothing wrong with you. Why, you may live forever; you have the body of a thirty-five-year-old. How old was your father when he died?"

"Did I say he was dead?" the patient asked.

The doctor was surprised and asked, "How old is he, and is he very active?"

"Well, he's eighty-one years old, still goes skiing a few times a season, and surfs three times a week during the summer," the patient replied.

The doctor couldn't believe it! So he asked, "Well, how old was your grandfather when he died?"

"Did I say he was dead?" asked the patient.

The doctor was astonished. He said, "You mean to tell me that you're sixty years old, and both your father and your grandfather are alive? Is your grandfather very active?"

"He goes skiing at least once a season and surfing once a week during the summer," explained the patient. "Not only that, he's one-hundred-and-two years old and he's getting married again next week."

A Guy Goes into a Doctor's Office. . .

"At one-hundred-and-two years of age, why on earth would he want to get married?" the doctor asked.

"Did I say he wanted to?" the man replied.

A Guy Goes into a Doctor's Office. . .

A man went to his doctor and complained that he was unable to do things around the house that he used to do.

After the doctor finished examining him, the man said, "OK, Doc, I can take it. Tell me in plain English what's wrong with me."

"Alright," the doctor replied, "in plain English, you're just lazy."

"OK," the man said. "Now tell me the medical term so I can tell my wife."

A woman goes into a doctor's office and yells out, "Kiss me, Doc, kiss me!"

The doctor looks at her and quietly replies, "It's against the code of ethics to kiss you."

Several minutes later the woman shouts out again, "Kiss me, Doc, please, kiss me just once!"

The doctor again refuses and says, "As a doctor, I simply cannot kiss you."

Finally, after another fifteen minutes, the woman pleads with the doctor, "Please, Doc, please, kiss me just once!"

"Listen," he says, "I am sorry, but I CANNOT kiss you. In fact, come to think of it, I probably shouldn't even be screwing you."

A man, dressed in a sterile gown and mask, was pacing up and down the hallway when the nurse came out of the room and approached him.

"The delivery is going very well," the nurse said. "Wouldn't you like to come in now?"

"No!" replied the man. "I can't stand all the blood and screaming. Leave me alone!"

A few minutes later the nurse came out again and said, "It's almost over. Wouldn't you like to come in now?"

"No! Leave me alone!" exclaimed the man. "I told you I cannot stand all that blood and screaming!"

"But you must," the nurse insisted. "The delivery is almost finished and you're the obstetrician."

While making his rounds with a group of medical students, the doctor draws their attention to an x-ray.

"As is clearly visible on the x-ray, the patient limps because her right fibula and tibia are radically arched. Mike, what would you do in a case like this?"

"Well, sir," says Mike, pondering the question, "I guess I'd limp, too."

Two doctors opened an office in a small town and put up a sign reading "Dr. Green and Dr. Jones, Psychiatry and Proctology."

The town council wasn't happy with the sign so the doctors changed it to "Hysterias and Posteriors."

This was unacceptable too, so in an effort to satisfy the council they changed the sign to "Schizoids and Hemorrhoids." Still no go.

Next they tried "Catatonics and High Colonics." Thumbs down again.

Then came "Manic-depressives and Anal Retentives." Still no good.

How about "Minds and Behinds?" Once more, unacceptable.

Next they tried "Lost Souls and Assholes." Still no go.

They even tried "Analysis and Anal Cysts," "Nuts and Butts," "Freaks and Cheeks," and "Loons and Moons," all of which were unacceptable.

Nearing their wit's end, the doctors finally came up with a business slogan they thought might be acceptable to the council: "Dr. Green and Dr. Jones, Odds and Ends." Approved.

A psychiatrist was making his usual morning rounds. When he entered one room, he found a patient sitting on the floor sawing a piece of wood with the side of his hand, and another hanging from the ceiling by his feet.

The doctor asked the patient sitting on the floor what he was doing. "Can't you see I'm sawing a piece of wood in half?" replied the patient, irritated by the doctor's question.

"And what is that fellow hanging from the ceiling doing?" inquired the doctor. "Oh, he's my friend," the patient replied, "but he is a little crazy. He thinks he's a lightbulb." "If he's your friend," the doctor said, "you should ask him to come down from there before he hurts himself."

"What?" the patient exclaimed. "And work in the dark?!?"

One day a family took their elderly, frail father to a nursing home with hopes that he would be well cared for.

The next day the nurses fed and bathed him and sat him in a chair by the window overlooking the beautiful flower garden. Everything seemed fine until a short time later when he began to fall over sideways in the chair.

Seeing this, two nurses immediately rushed over to him and straightened him up in the chair. Shortly thereafter he began to tilt to the other side. Once more the nurses rushed over and straightened him up. This routine went on for the entire morning.

Later in the day his family arrived to see how he was adjusting to his new environment. "So, Dad, how are things going here? Are they treating you well?" they asked him.

"It's pretty nice," he replied, "but they won't let you fart!"

A young doctor doing his residency in OB/GYN felt embarrassed while performing a female pelvic exam. To cover his embarrassment he had unconsciously formed a habit of whistling softly.

While he was performing this exam on a middle-aged lady, she suddenly burst out laughing. This only furthered his embarrassment.

"Just what do you find so amusing, madam?" he snarled.

"I'm so sorry, doctor," she replied, "but the song you were whistling was . . . 'I wish I was an Oscar Meyer Wiener'!"

A guy goes into a psychiatrist's office dressed as an American Indian, screaming "Doc, Doc, you've got to help me. I'm all confused. One day I wake up thinking I'm a wigwam, the next day I wake up thinking I'm a teepee." The psychiatrist says, "Calm down, relax, I know what your problem is." "You do?" says the Indian hopefully. "Sure," says the psychiatrist. "You're two tents."

"Doctor," the embarrassed man said, "I have a sexual problem. I can't get it up for my wife anymore."

"Mr. Thomas, bring her back with you tomorrow and let me see what I can do."

So the worried fellow returned with his wife the following day. The doctor greeted the couple and then said, "Please remove your clothes, Mrs. Thomas." The woman obliged and removed her clothing. "OK, now turn all the way around . . . Now, lie down please . . . Uh-huh, I see. Alright, you can put your clothes back on."

While the woman was busy dressing herself again, the doctor took the husband aside. "You're in perfect health," he said to the man. "Your wife didn't give me an erection either."

In a long line of people waiting for a bank teller, one guy suddenly started massaging the back of the person in front of him. Surprised, the man in front turned and snarled, "Just what the hell are you doing?"

"Well," said the guy, "you see, I'm a chiropractor and I could tell that you were tense, so I thought I'd massage your back."

"That's the stupidest thing I've ever heard!" the guy replied. "I work for the IRS. Do you see me screwing the guy in front of me?"

A Guy Goes into a Doctor's Office. . .

Three doctors met at a party, and it wasn't long until the conversation got around to their specialties and what kind of cars they drove.

"I'm a veterinarian," said the first fellow. "So, naturally, I drive a white 'Vette."

As they smiled and nodded, the second man said, "I'm an obstetrician, so I drive an Accord."

Now the third guy was quiet until he was egged on by the other two.

"Well," he finally said, "I'm a proctologist . . . and I have a brown Probe."

A plastic surgeon was getting ready to perform a little tuck on a middle-aged woman. He noticed that she was a little nervous, so he began to tell her a story as he was putting on his surgical gloves.

"Do you know how they make these rubber gloves?"

She said, "No."

"Well," he spoofed, "down in Mexico they have this big building set up with a large tank of latex, and the workers are all picked according to hand size. Each individual walks up to the tank, dips their hands in, and then walks around for a bit while the latex sets up and dries right onto their hands! Then they peel off the gloves and throw them into the big 'Finished Goods' crate and start the process all over again."

The nervous woman didn't laugh a bit! Five minutes later, just before she was going under anesthesia, she burst out laughing, blushed, and exclaimed, "I just thought about how they must make condoms!"

Three patients in a mental institution prepare for an examination given by the head psychiatrist. If the patients pass the exam they will be free to leave the hospital. If they fail, however, the institution will detain them for five more years.

The doctor takes the three patients to the top of a diving board over an empty swimming pool and asks the first patient to jump.

The first patient jumps head first into the pool and breaks both arms.

The second patient jumps and breaks both legs.

The third patient looks over the side and refuses to jump.

"Congratulations! You're a free man. Just tell me, why you didn't jump?" asked the doctor.

"Well, Doc, I can't swim!"

Two psychiatrists were at a convention. As they conversed over a drink, one asked, "What was your most difficult case?"

The other replied, "I had a patient who lived in a pure fantasy world. He believed that an uncle in South America was going to die and leave him a fortune. All day long he waited for a letter to arrive from an attorney. He never went out, he never did anything; he merely sat around and waited for this fantasy letter from this fantasy uncle."

"What was the result?" the first doctor asked.

"It was an eight-year struggle. Every day for eight years, but I finally cured him. And then that stupid letter arrived!"

A businessman was feeling very ill and went to the doctor. The doctor examined him and backed away saying, "I'm sorry to tell you this, but you have an advanced case of highly infectious rabies. You must have had it for some time. It will almost certainly be fatal."

"Could you give me a pen and paper?" asked the businessman.

"Do you want to write your will?" asked the doctor.

"No, I want to make a list of all the people I want to bite!"

A doctor at an insane asylum decided to take the inmates to a baseball game. For weeks in advance he coached his patients to respond to his commands. When the day of the game arrived, everything seemed to be going well.

As the national anthem started, the doctor yelled, "Up, nuts!" The inmates complied by standing up.

After the anthem he yelled, "Down, nuts!" They all sat.

After a home run he yelled, "Cheer, nuts!" They all broke into applause and cheers.

Thinking things were going very well, he decided to go get a beer and a hot dog, leaving his assistant in charge. When he returned there was a riot in progress.

Finding his assistant, he asked what happened. The assistant replied, "Well . . . everything was fine until some guy walked by and yelled, 'PEANUTS!'"

*WHAT DOCTORS SAY
(WHAT DOCTOR'S THINK)

• "This should be taken care of right away."
(I'd planned a trip to Hawaii next month but this is so easy and profitable that I want to fix it before it cures itself.)

• "Well, what have we here . . .?"
(He has no idea and is hoping you'll give him a clue.)

• "Let me check your medical history."
(I want to see if you have paid your last bill before spending any more time with you.)

• "Why don't we make another appointment later in the week?"
(I'm playing golf this afternoon and this is a waste of time.) or (I need the bucks, so I'm charging you for another office visit.)

• "We have some good news and some bad news."
(The good news is I'm going to buy that new BMW. The bad news is you're going to pay for it.)

A Guy Goes into a Doctor's Office. . .

• "Let's see how it develops."
(Maybe in a few days it will grow into something that can be cured.)

• "Let me schedule you for some tests."
(I have a 40% interest in the lab.)

• "I'd like to have my associate look at you."
(He's going through a messy divorce and owes me a bundle.)

• "I'd like to prescribe a new drug."
(I'm writing a paper and would like to use you for a guinea pig.)

• "If it doesn't clear up in a week, give me a call."
(I don't know what it is. Maybe it will go away by itself.)

After a baby was born, the panicked Japanese father went to see the obstetrician. "Doctor," he said, "I'm a little upset because my daughter has red hair. She can't possibly be mine."

"Nonsense," the doctor said. "Even though you and your wife both have black hair, one of your ancestors may have contributed red hair to the gene pool." "It isn't possible," the man insisted. "We're pure Japanese."

"Well," said the doctor, "let me ask you this. How often do you have sex?"

The man seemed ashamed. "I've been working very hard for the past year. We only make love once or twice a month."

"There you have it!" the doctor said confidently. "It's just rust."

A hurricane blew across the Caribbean. It didn't take long for an expensive yacht to be swamped by high waves and sink without a trace. There were only two survivors: the boat's owner, Dr. Goldstein, and its steward, Benny, who managed to swim to the closest island.

After reaching the deserted strip of land, the steward was crying and very upset that they would never be found. The doctor was quite calm, relaxing against a tree.

"Dr. Goldstein, Dr. Goldstein, how can you be so calm?" cried Benny. "We're going to die on this lonely island. We'll never be discovered here."

"Sit down and listen to what I have to say, Benny," began the confident Dr. Goldstein. "Five years ago I gave the United Way $500,000, and another $500,000 to the United Jewish Appeal. I donated the same amounts four years ago. And three years ago, since I did very well in the stock market, I contributed $750,000 to each. Last year business was good, so the two charities each got $1,000,000 dollars."

"So what?" shouted Benny.

"Well, it's time for their annual fund drives. They'll find me!"

A physician visited a mental institution and asked a patient, "How did you get here? What is the nature of your illness?"

He got this reply: "It started when I got married, and I guess I should never have done it. I got hitched to a widow with a grown daughter, who then became my stepdaughter. My daddy came to visit us, fell in love with my lovely stepdaughter, then married her. And so my stepdaughter was now my stepmother. Soon my wife had a son who was, of course, my daddy's brother-in-law since he is the half-brother of my stepdaughter, who is now, of course, my daddy's wife. So, as I told you, my stepdaughter married my daddy, so she became my stepmother. Now since my new son is brother to my stepmother, he also became my uncle."

"As you know, my wife is my step-grandmother since she is my stepmother's mother. Don't forget that my stepmother is my stepdaughter. Remember, too, that I am my wife's grandson."

"But hold on just a few minutes more, you see, since I'm married to my step-grandmother, I am not only my wife's grandson and her hubby, but I am also my own grandfather."

"Now, can you understand how I got in this place?"

A Guy Goes into a Doctor's Office. . .

A man walked into a doctor's office. "What do you have?" the receptionist asked him. "Shingles," he replied. She told him to sit down.

Soon a nurse came in and asked, "What do you have?" "Shingles," he replied.

She took his blood pressure, weight, and complete medical history. Then she took him to a room, told him to remove all of his clothes, and left. After a few minutes the doctor came in and asked, "What do you have?" "Shingles," the man told him.

The doctor looked him up and down and asked, "Where? I don't see them."

"Out on the truck. Where do you want me to unload them?"

"QUICKIES"

• Patient: Doctor, you've got to help me. I think I'm a kleptomaniac.
Doctor: Don't worry. I think there's something you can take for that.

• Doctors bury their mistakes.

• As a doctor was examining his patient, he asked, "Any coughing, wheezing, or shortness of cash?"

• Why did the proctologist use two fingers?
In case the patient wanted a second opinion.

• Why do women prefer old gynecologists?
They have shaky hands!

A new medical facility with several different specialists opened in a trendy part of the city. Wanting to be different and creative, the administration decided that each doctor's office door would, in some way, be representative of his practice.

So, when construction was complete . . . the eye doctor's door had a peep hole, the orthopedist's door had a broken hinge, the psychiatrist's door was painted all kinds of crazy colors, and the proctologist's door was left open . . . just a crack.

At a big cocktail party, an obstetrician's wife noticed another guest was making overtures to her husband. But it was a large, informal gathering, so she tried to laugh it off—until she saw them disappear into a bedroom together.

All at once she rushed into the room, pulled the two apart and screamed, "Look, lady! My husband just delivers babies, he doesn't install them!"

A woman went to see her doctor. When he inquired about her complaint she replied that she suffered from a discharge. He instructed her to get undressed and lie down on the examining table. She did so. The doctor put on rubber gloves and began to massage her "private parts."

After a couple of minutes he asked, "How does that feel?"

"Wonderful," she replied, "but the discharge is in my ear."

A doctor at the beginning of an examination placed his stethoscope on an elderly and slightly deaf female patient's posterior chest wall. "Big breaths," instructed the doctor.

"Yes, they used to be," responded the patient with remorse.

A guy goes into a doctor's office and has some questions, so he says, "Every time I go on vacation, my wife gets pregnant. Went to France and she got pregnant. Went to Ireland and she got pregnant a second time. Went to Spain and she got pregnant a third time."

The doctor says, "Have you ever thought of using any kind of protection to avoid it?"

The man says, "No, I just thought that maybe next time I'd take my wife with me."

A psychiatrist's secretary walks into his study and says, "There's a gentleman in the waiting room asking to see you. Claims he's invisible."

The psychiatrist responds, "Tell him I can't see him."

A beautiful young lady in a dentist's chair was nervously wringing her hands. "Oh, dear," she said, "I'm so nervous. It's so frightening. I think I'd rather have a baby than have my teeth worked on."

"Well," replied the dentist, "which would you like the most? Just let me know and I'll adjust the chair accordingly."

A Guy Goes into a Doctor's Office. . .

A fellow was sitting in the doctor's waiting room and said to himself every so often, "Lord, I hope I'm sick!"

After about the fifth or sixth time, the receptionist couldn't stand it any longer and asked, "Why in the world would you want to be sick, Mr. Adams?"

The man replied, "I'd hate to be well and feel as lousy as this."

A plastic surgeon and his wife were sunbathing on a beach when a well-endowed, beautiful, young, blonde woman in a tight-fitting bikini strolled passed. The woman looked at the doctor, smiled seductively, and said in a very sexy voice, "Hi there, handsome. How are you doing?" then wiggled her backside and walked off.

"Who was that?!" demanded the doctor's wife.

"Er—just a woman I met professionally," replied the doctor.

"Oh, yeah?!" snarled the wife. "In whose profession, yours or hers?!"

A new nurse listened while the doctor was yelling, "Typhoid! Tetanus! Measles!"

The new nurse asked another nurse, "Why is he doing that?"

The other nurse replied, "Oh, he just likes to call the shots around here."

A doctor entered the waiting room. "I have some good news for you, Mrs. Peterson."

"Pardon me," she interrupted, "but it's 'Miss'."

The doctor said, "I have some bad news for you, Miss Peterson."

"I can't find a cause for your illness," the doctor said. "Frankly, I think it's due to drinking."

"In that case," replied his patient, "I'll come back when you are sober."

A Guy Goes into a Doctor's Office. . .

A man asked his doctor if he thought he'd live to be a hundred. The doctor asked the man, "Do you smoke or drink?"

"No," he replied, "I've never done either."

"Do you gamble, drive fast cars, or fool around with women?" inquired the doctor.

"No, I've never done any of those things either."

"Well then," said the doctor, "why do you want to live to be a hundred?"

A woman went to her doctor for a follow-up visit after the doctor had prescribed testosterone for her. She was a little worried about some of the side effects she was experiencing. "Doctor, the male hormones you've been giving me have really helped, but I'm afraid that you're giving me too much. I've started growing hair in places that I've never grown hair before."

The doctor reassured her. "A little hair growth is a perfectly normal side effect of testosterone. Just where has this hair appeared?"

"On my balls."

Albert walks in to his doctor's office for his yearly physical exam as he has done every year that he can remember. The doctor takes him through all of the motions, does the normal tests, and then leaves to get the results. After about fifteen minutes the doctor returns with a very sad look on his face.

"Well, Doc, what kind of shape am I in this time?" Albert asks.

"Albert, I don't know what to say. The news is bad. Really bad," says the doctor.

"What is it, Doc?" asks Albert.

"I hate to have to give you such bad news. I can't find the words to tell you. I really don't know what to say."

Albert, being a strong man who appreciates straight talk, tells the doctor, "OK, don't beat around the bush. Tell me what you know. I can take it."

"Well," says the doctor, "let me put it this way. I think that you should go to Arkansas and visit the hot springs there for a nice relaxing mud bath. Spend some time soaking in the mud."

"Oh, so I need to relax a little bit, eh? Will that cure me, Doc?" asked Albert.

"No Albert, it won't cure you. And it may not help you relax. But it will help you get used to being covered in dirt."

The doctor has just finished examining a very attractive young girl.

"Have you been going out with men?" he asks.

"Oh no, Doctor, never!"

"Are you quite sure? Bearing in mind that I've fully examined you, do you still say you've never had anything to do with men?"

"Quite sure, Doctor."

The doctor immediately runs to the window and looks up. The girl says, "What are you doing?"

The doctor says, "Well, the last time this happened a star arose in the East."

Patient: "Doctor, I'm very worried. I'm still suffering from exhaustion and fatigue when I come home from work every evening."

Doctor: "Oh, that's nothing to worry about. Just have a few drinks before your dinner—that will soon wake you up."

Patient: "Thanks very much, Doctor! But when I consulted you before, you told me to cut out drinking alcohol completely."

Doctor: "Yes, so I did. But that was last week, old chap—and medical science has progressed enormously since then."

Suffering from a bad case of the flu, the outraged patient bellowed, "Three weeks? The doctor can't see me for three weeks? I could well be dead by then!"

Calmly, the voice at the other end of the line replied, "If so, would you call to cancel the appointment."

A Guy Goes into a Doctor's Office. . .

A guy had been feeling down for so long that he finally decided to seek the aid of a psychiatrist.

He went there, lay on the couch, spilled his guts, then waited for the profound wisdom of the psychiatrist to make him feel better.

The psychiatrist asked him a few questions, took some notes, then sat thinking in silence for a few minutes with a puzzled look on his face.

Suddenly he looked up with an expression of delight and said, "Um, I think your problem is low self-esteem. It is very common among losers."

An optometrist was instructing a new employee on how to charge a customer:

"As you are fitting his glasses, if he asks how much they cost, you say $75.00 . . ."

If his eyes don't flutter, say, "For the frames. The lenses will be $50.00 . . ."

If his eyes still don't flutter, you add ". . .each."

A Guy Goes into a Doctor's Office. . .

An orthopedic supply salesman was delivering a display skeleton to a doctor. He sat the skeleton in the passenger seat of the car with his bony arm across the back of the seat.

He hadn't considered the drive across town. At one traffic light the stares of the people in the car beside him became obvious, and he looked across and explained, "I'm delivering him to a doctor's office."

The other driver leaned out of his window. "I hate to tell you, buddy," he said, "but I think it's too late!"

While visiting a friend who was in the hospital, a man noticed several pretty nurses, each of whom was wearing a pin designed to look like an apple.

He asked one nurse what the pin signified.

"Nothing," she said with a smile. "It's just to keep the doctors away."

A Guy Goes into a Doctor's Office. . .

A pretty young blonde visiting her new doctor for the first time found herself alone in a small waiting room. She began undressing nervously, preparing herself for the upcoming examination. Just as she draped the last of her garments over the back of a chair, a light rap sounded on the door and a young doctor strode in.

Coming to an abrupt halt, the doctor looked his nude patient up and down carefully and with considerable appreciation.

"Miss Smith," he said finally, "it seems quite obvious to me that until today you have never undergone an eye examination."

A Guy Goes into a Doctor's Office. . .

Two women were sitting in the doctor's waiting room comparing notes on their various disorders.

"I want a baby more than anything in the world," said the first, "but I guess it is impossible."

"I used to feel just the same way," said the second. "But then everything changed. That's why I'm here. I'm going to have a baby in three months."

"You must tell me what you did."

"I went to a faith healer."

"But I've tried that. My husband and I went to one for nearly a year and it didn't help a bit."

The other woman smiled and whispered, "Try going alone next time, dearie."

A Guy Goes into a Doctor's Office...

A worried father telephoned his family doctor and said that he was afraid that his teenaged son had come down with an S.T.D. "He says he hasn't had sex with anyone but the maid, so it has to be her."

"Don't worry so much," advised the doctor. "These things happen."

"I know, Doctor," said the father, "but I have to admit that I've been sleeping with the maid also. I seem to have the same symptoms."

"That's unfortunate."

"Not only that, I think I've passed it on to my wife."

"Oh, God," said the doc, "that means we all have it."

A patient complained to his doctor, "I've been to three other doctors and none of them agreed with your diagnosis."

The doctor calmly replied, "Just wait until your autopsy, then they'll see that I was right."

A Guy Goes into a Doctor's Office. . .

A man decides to take the opportunity while his wife is away to paint the toilet seat. The wife comes home sooner than expected, sits, and gets the seat stuck to her rear.

She is understandably distraught about this and asks her husband to drive her to the doctor. She puts on a large overcoat so as to cover the stuck seat, and they go. When they get to the doctor's, the man lifts his wife's coat to show their predicament. The man asks, "Doctor, have you ever seen anything like this before?"

"Well, yes," the doctor replies, "but never framed."

A professor of medicine, a man well-known for his earnest and oft-proclaimed views on temperance, was lecturing his medical students on the damage that alcohol can do. To demonstrate its effect on the nervous system, he took a worm and dropped it into a glass of gin and tonic. The worm wiggled around for a few minutes before finally giving a few convulsive twitches and dying.

"And can we deduce anything from that?" asked the professor with a triumphant air, implying that only an obvious conclusion could be drawn.

"Yes," came a voice from the back, "if you've got worms, drink alcohol."

Doctors were asked to consider contributing to the construction of a new wing at the hospital. What did they do?

The allergists voted to scratch it.

The dermatologists preferred no rash moves.

The gastroenterologists had a gut feeling about it.

The neurologists thought the administration had a lot of nerve.

The obstetricians stated they were laboring under a misconception.

The ophthalmologists considered the idea short sighted.

The orthopedists issued a joint resolution.

The pathologists yelled, "Over my dead body!"

The pediatricians said, "Grow up."

The proctologists said, "We are in arrears."

The psychiatrists thought it was madness.

The surgeons decided to wash their hands of the whole thing.

The radiologists could see right through it.

The internists thought it was a hard pill to swallow.

The plastic surgeons said, "This puts a whole
   new face on the matter."
The podiatrists thought it was a big step forward.
The urologists felt the scheme wouldn't hold
   water.
The cardiologists didn't have the heart to say no.

A doctor and a lawyer were talking at a party. Their conversation was constantly interrupted by people describing their ailments and asking the doctor for free medical advice. After an hour of this, the exasperated doctor asked the lawyer, "What do you do to stop people from asking you for legal advice when you're out of the office?"

"I give it to them," replied the lawyer, "and then I send them a bill."

The doctor was shocked but agreed to give it a try. The next day, still feeling slightly guilty, the doctor prepared the bills. When he went to place them in his mailbox, he found a bill from the lawyer.

Dr. Jones, a young psychiatrist, begins his practice in an office building. After several weeks he realizes that the older man he usually sees in the elevator each morning and evening is Dr. Smith, also a psychiatrist. Finally, after a month or two of frequently sharing the elevator, Dr. Jones pulls his skewed tie, rakes his fingers through his disarrayed hair, and approaches his colleague. "Dr. Smith," he says. "Every day I step into this elevator in the evening, exhausted and frazzled by the gut-wrenching stories of my patients, while you appear as calm and cool as you do each morning. Tell me, please, how do you do it? How do you maintain your equanimity after listening to the woes of your patients?" "My dear Dr. Jones," replied the older man. "Who says I listen?"

A Guy Goes into a Doctor's Office...

A surgeon and a family physician went on a fishing trip in Wyoming. Upon returning to their camp early one evening, they were confronted by an enraged grizzly bear. The surgeon quickly dropped to one knee to begin lacing up his running shoes. Inching backward, as the bear drew ever closer, the family doctor muttered to the surgeon, "As I calculate it, we can never outrun this bear!" The surgeon looked up only to retort, " As I calculate it, all I have to do is out-run you!"

A student with a love for biology, particularly dissection, entered medical school and announced that he wanted to become a coroner. His student advisor asked him why he would choose that specialty.

"Well," he replied, "I want to operate on people, but I don't want their lives to depend on it."

A Guy Goes into a Doctor's Office. . .

An elderly woman went to her monthly doctor appointment and complained to the nurse about the long delays she always endures.

When her name was finally called, she was asked to step on the scale. "I need to get your weight today," said the nurse.

Without a moment's hesitation, the woman replied, "One hour and forty-five minutes."

A woman in her nineties is distraught after the death of her warm, caring, faithful husband of seventy years. She can't live without him and decides that the best way to do herself in is to stab herself in her broken heart. Still, she doesn't want to linger, so she calls a doctor to find out exactly where the heart is. He tells her to put her first two fingers together, hold them horizontally and place the tip of the first finger just below her left nipple. The heart, he says, is immediately below the first knuckle on her second finger.

Later that day, the doctor is called to the emergency room to put fourteen stitches in the elderly woman's left thigh.

A rich businessman's wife broke her hip. The businessman got the best bone surgeon in the country to do the operation, which consisted of lining up the broken hip and putting in a screw to secure it. The operation went fine, and the doctor sent the businessman a bill for his fee of $5,000. The businessman was outraged and sent the doctor a letter demanding an itemized list of the costs. The doctor sent back a list with two items:

1 screw – $1.00
Knowing how to put it in – $4,999.00

An artist asked the gallery owner if anyone had shown interest in his paintings. "I've got good news and bad news," she said. "The good news is that some guy inquired if they would appreciate in value after you died. When I told him they would, he bought all fifteen of your paintings."

"And the bad news?"

"The guy was your doctor."

There once was a doctor who was so conceited about his looks and charm that whenever he took a woman's pulse, he subtracted ten beats to account for her excitement at being near him.

If it's dry, add moisture. If it's moistened, add dryness. Congratulations—now you're a dermatologist!